# THIS IS ME! ACROSTICS

## Amazing Verses

Edited By Wendy Laws

First published in Great Britain in 2022 by:

Young Writers
Remus House
Coltsfoot Drive
Peterborough
PE2 9BF
Telephone: 01733 890066
Website: www.youngwriters.co.uk

All Rights Reserved
Book Design by Ashley Janson
© Copyright Contributors 2022
Softback ISBN 978-1-83928-602-5

Printed and bound in the UK by BookPrintingUK
Website: www.bookprintinguk.com
YB0519A

# Foreword

Welcome Reader,

For Young Writers' latest competition *This Is Me Acrostics*, we asked primary school pupils to look inside themselves, to think about what makes them unique, and then write an acrostic poem about it! They rose to the challenge magnificently and the result is this fantastic collection of poems, celebrating them and the things that are important to them.

Here at Young Writers our aim is to encourage creativity in children and to inspire a love of the written word, so it's great to get such an amazing response, with some absolutely fantastic poems. It's important for children to focus on and celebrate themselves and this competition allowed them to write freely and honestly, celebrating what makes them great, expressing their hopes and fears, or simply writing about their favourite things. *This Is Me Acrostics* gave them the power of words.

I'd like to congratulate all the young poets in this anthology, I hope this inspires them to continue with their creative writing.

# Contents

**Independent Entries**

| | |
|---|---|
| Misaki (6) | 1 |

**Bearbrook Combined School, Aylesbury**

| | |
|---|---|
| Lacey Tarling (7) | 2 |
| Aayaan Pandey (7) | 3 |
| Idrees Akram (6) | 4 |
| Adam Kralik (7) | 5 |
| Hamza Alyas (6) | 6 |
| Finley Rogers (7) | 7 |
| Daisy Cox (6) | 8 |
| Tommy Coward (7) | 9 |
| Jonny McFetrich (7) | 10 |
| Fanta Camara (7) | 11 |
| Fazia Zahid (7) | 12 |
| Deyana K | 13 |
| Poppy Baldwin (7) | 14 |
| Niamh Garvey (6) | 15 |
| Alexander Da Silva (7) | 16 |
| Summer Grew (7) | 17 |
| Mia Domagala (6) | 18 |

**Briary Primary School, Herne Bay**

| | |
|---|---|
| Matthew Biagi (7) | 19 |
| Archie Moulton (6) | 20 |
| Eli Offormezle (7) | 21 |
| Immanuel Osagie (7) | 22 |
| Poppy Gaute (6) | 23 |
| Tillie Griggs (6) | 24 |
| Phoebe Goldstraw (7) | 25 |
| Amber Arnold (6) | 26 |
| Minsa Reman (7) | 27 |

| | |
|---|---|
| Liam Allen (6) | 28 |
| Theo Cooley (5) | 29 |
| MJ Wheeler (6) | 30 |
| Max Johnson (7) | 31 |
| Aubrey Hornsey (6) | 32 |
| Max Hart (6) | 33 |
| Jack Brookes (7) | 34 |
| Taylor Clark-Jones (7) | 35 |
| Jessica Kelly (7) | 36 |
| Lillie-Mae Guida (6) | 37 |
| Poppy Tambling (6) | 38 |
| Blaze Blackwood (6) | 39 |
| Evie-Sue Weller (6) | 40 |
| Logan Bennett (7) | 41 |
| Harper Robb (6) | 42 |
| Jaxon Wells | 43 |
| Elyshia Lee (7) | 44 |
| Anuja Sawade (6) | 45 |
| Bella Guly (6) | 46 |
| Jamsine Warren-Davies (7) | 47 |
| Chloe Osbourn (6) | 48 |
| Callum O'Shea (6) | 49 |
| Maisie-Anne Arnold (7) | 50 |
| Loki Read (7) | 51 |
| Joey Dalten-Bower | 52 |
| Elsie Gray (7) | 53 |
| Daisy Hillier (5) | 54 |

**Chilham St Mary's CE Primary School, Chilham**

| | |
|---|---|
| Olive Eaves (7) | 55 |
| Eleana Barton Slade (7) | 56 |
| Poppy Atkin (6) | 57 |
| Martha Wright (5) | 58 |
| Phoebe Shoults (7) | 59 |

## Emersons Green Primary School, Emersons Green

| | |
|---|---|
| Autumn Millard (6) | 60 |
| Archie Savage (6) | 61 |
| Imani May Teddy (6) | 62 |
| Sofia Beard (6) | 63 |
| Alba Davey (6) | 64 |

## Goodyers End Primary School, Bedworth

| | |
|---|---|
| Kelisia Mellis (7) | 65 |
| Tamara Adeyemo (4) | 66 |
| Robyn Rule (5) | 67 |
| Riley Barson (5) | 68 |
| Dylan Savage (6) | 69 |
| Ariel Nwagwu (7) | 70 |
| Thomas Lewis (6) | 71 |
| Siya Yadav (5) | 72 |
| Ranjot Singh (7) | 73 |
| Maisie Gleeson (4) | 74 |
| Alexis Nwagwu (7) | 75 |

## Holy Cross RC Primary School, Fulham

| | |
|---|---|
| Carlos Etayo Sanchez (5) | 76 |
| Hesham Dajani (6) | 77 |
| Eden Assefa (6) | 78 |
| Hannah Macias (6) | 79 |
| Claudia Nortes (7) | 80 |
| Isabella Newell (7) | 81 |
| Jessica Osorio Tavares (7) | 82 |
| Amelia Lovett (5) | 83 |
| Benjamin Smith (7) | 84 |
| Adewunmi (7) | 85 |
| Hallie Morgan (5) | 86 |
| Leila Nuqui (6) | 87 |
| Viktoria Hoxha (6) | 88 |
| Valery Astaiza (6) | 89 |
| Amen Benyam (7) | 90 |
| Jacob Duffield (7) | 91 |
| Zach Wyatt (6) | 92 |
| Oliver Dobbs (6) & Teresa | 93 |
| Nina Ribeiro Hill (6) | 94 |
| Mason Kirby-Taylor (5) | 95 |
| Blanca Solans (6) | 96 |
| Alexander Bracke (6) | 97 |
| Elnathan Elias (6) | 98 |
| Arthur Charles Farrell Dewfall (6) | 99 |
| Evelina Juncu (6) & Sara (6) | 100 |
| Romano Mason (6) | 101 |
| Kitty Hughes (6) | 102 |
| Marcela Marcatto de Abreu (6) | 103 |
| Paul Patrick Lloyd (6) | 104 |
| Luna Petrillo (6) | 105 |
| Harrison Mbilika-Edafioka (6) | 106 |
| Sebastian (6) | 107 |
| Constance (6) | 108 |
| Isabel Fontes Cardoso (6) | 109 |
| Conor Byrne (6) | 110 |
| Alex Frain (7) | 111 |
| Leandro Pyaralli Salvador (6) | 112 |
| Joseph Jackson (7) | 113 |
| Noah McGuirk (6) | 114 |
| Afonso (5) | 115 |
| Felix Ihlenfeld (6) | 116 |
| Maisy Power (6) | 117 |
| Foucauld Gaudy (6) | 118 |

## Marlcliffe Community Primary School, Sheffield

| | |
|---|---|
| Jenny O'Brien (5) | 119 |
| Dexter Bott (7) | 120 |
| Poppy Sweeney (7) | 121 |
| Zoe Nall (6) | 122 |
| Georgia Neasmith (7) | 123 |
| Harriet Grayson (6) | 124 |
| Alice Hague (6) | 125 |
| Theo Brown (7) | 126 |
| Darcie Thompson (7) | 127 |
| Matilda Stone (7) | 128 |
| Jesse Akers (7) | 129 |
| Amelie Callaghan (7) | 130 |
| River Savage (6) | 131 |

| | |
|---|---|
| Ava Bothamley (7) | 132 |
| Dominic Hague (7) | 133 |
| Anna Brownley (6) | 134 |
| Emmiie Perry (7) | 135 |
| Lenny Anglesea-French (6) | 136 |

## Purbrook Infant School, Purbrook

| | |
|---|---|
| Jacob Leither (6) | 137 |
| Lilly-Anne Fry (7) | 138 |
| Darcie Ellcome (7) | 139 |
| Scarlett Wright (7) | 140 |
| Cusin Aji Joseph (7) | 141 |
| Isla Dalgleish (6) | 142 |
| Hayden Jackson (7) | 143 |
| Charlie Shepherd (7) | 144 |
| Sienna Gosden (7) | 145 |
| Angel Bailey (7) | 146 |
| Sophia Cork (7) | 147 |
| Mason Saunders (7) | 148 |
| Logan Martin (7) | 149 |
| Holly Ziya (7) | 150 |

## St Mary's Catholic Primary School, London

| | |
|---|---|
| Rayan Bouje Llaba (7) | 151 |
| Maria Pinnock (7) | 152 |
| Soraiya Borelly (6) | 153 |
| Nayomi Solomon (7) | 154 |
| Kamber Tanai (7) | 155 |
| Livia Moscatelli-Darroux (6) | 156 |
| Jeremiah Komeh (6) | 157 |

## St Michael's CE (Aided) Primary School, Tettenhall

| | |
|---|---|
| Sraiyah Holmes (6) | 158 |
| Gureet Tutt (6) | 159 |
| Oliver Clarkson (6) | 160 |
| Nathan Nurse (6) | 161 |
| Etta Tillett (5) | 162 |
| Hirah Saeed (5) | 163 |
| Rowan Douglas (6) | 164 |
| Shahin Khaja (6) | 165 |
| Carter Bailey (5) | 166 |
| Lucas Bromley (5) | 167 |
| Jaxon Durnall (5) | 168 |
| Mary Evans (6) | 169 |
| Lexi Bowen (5) | 170 |
| Pearl Brown (6) | 171 |
| Noah Jimenez-Kaul (6) | 172 |
| Avni Puri (6) | 173 |
| Aila Brown (6) | 174 |
| Jap Sidhu (6) | 175 |

# The Acrostics

# Misaki

**M** y name is Japanese.
**I** love to run.
**S** ometimes I play with Mummy.
**A** fter school, I like to read.
**K** ind people play with me.
**I** have two cats and a dog.

**Misaki (6)**

# Winter

W inter, I was born in the winter.
I have a dog and I love him.
N ow I am going to be eight in November.
T arling is my last name.
E lephants are big.
R hinos are as big as an elephant.

## Lacey Tarling (7)
Bearbrook Combined School, Aylesbury

# Orange

**O** range is my favourite colour.
**R** anger game puts on labour.
**A** pple is my favourite fruit.
**N** o I don't like oats.
**G** reen is my favourite colour.
**E** very day I play with my sister.

**Aayaan Pandey (7)**
Bearbrook Combined School, Aylesbury

# Idrees

**I** drees loves playing football.
**D** ad plays with me.
**R** ed is my favourite colour.
**E** very day I play football.
**E** very day I go to school.
**S** picy noodles I eat.

## Idrees Akram (6)
Bearbrook Combined School, Aylesbury

# Collie

C ollie is my favourite dog.
O is my favourite letter.
L ike football.
L ike fried chicken.
I saac is my best friend.
E gypt is a good country!

**Adam Kralik (7)**
Bearbrook Combined School, Aylesbury

# Hamza

**H** yenas are one of my favourite animals.
**A** pteranodon is one of my favourite animals.
**M** y cousin is kind.
**Z** is in my name.
**A** T-rex is scary.

## Hamza Alyas (6)
Bearbrook Combined School, Aylesbury

# Happy

**H** ome is my favourite place.
**A** nice and warm place.
**P** laying all the time.
**P** otatoes are my favourite food.
**Y** ellow is my favourite colour.

**Finley Rogers (7)**
Bearbrook Combined School, Aylesbury

# Happy

H ot day at the seaside.
A pples are nice and juicy.
P oppy is my friend.
P laytime is the best.
Y oghurt is my favourite dessert.

## Daisy Cox (6)
Bearbrook Combined School, Aylesbury

# Smart

**S** omerset is my favourite place.
**M** y best friend is Nathan
**A** nd I am so happy.
**R** unning is my favourite sport.
**T** ommy is my name.

**Tommy Coward (7)**
Bearbrook Combined School, Aylesbury

# Jonny

**J** elly and Nutella taste nice.
**O** range and red are my favourite colours.
**N** ice and funny.
**N** uts are hard.
**Y** oghurt is yummy.

## Jonny McFetrich (7)
Bearbrook Combined School, Aylesbury

# Fanta

**F** unny and kind.
**A** pples are my favourite fruit.
**N** utella tastes nice.
**T** V is sometimes boring.
**A** mango is my favourite.

**Fanta Camara (7)**
Bearbrook Combined School, Aylesbury

# Money

**M** y friends are fast.
**O** ranges are amazing.
**N** o one is annoying.
**E** x best friends.
**Y** ou are respectful.

## Fazia Zahid (7)
Bearbrook Combined School, Aylesbury

# Horse

**H** ow do I do?
**O** ther types.
**R** acing car.
**S** nakes are dangerous.
**E** lephant.

**Deyana K**
Bearbrook Combined School, Aylesbury

# Dog

**D** ogs are my favourite pet.
**O** range is my favourite colour.
**G** inger is a dog's colour.

## Poppy Baldwin (7)
Bearbrook Combined School, Aylesbury

# Red

**R** eading is my favourite.
**E** ggs are my favourite food.
**D** ucks are my favourite animal.

**Niamh Garvey (6)**
Bearbrook Combined School, Aylesbury

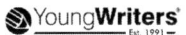

# Red

R eading is my favourite.
E ggs are my favourite.
D yeing my hair I don't like.

## Alexander Da Silva (7)
Bearbrook Combined School, Aylesbury

# One

O ne of my favourite things to do is draw,
N ext is to read.
E legant and fun.

## Summer Grew (7)
Bearbrook Combined School, Aylesbury

# Mia

**M** y name is Mia.
**I** like strawberry ice cream.
**A** silly person I am!

## Mia Domagala (6)
Bearbrook Combined School, Aylesbury

# Matthew Biagi

**M** atch with Mum's hair colour.
**A** big brother chasing me.
**T** all house.
**T** he beach is my favourite.
**H** ot days are great.
**E** very day I'll be kind.
**W** aves are great on the beach.

**B** athing on the beach is good.
**I** like riding trains.
**A** day at the beach.
**G** entle with everything.
**I** love going to school.

## Matthew Biagi (7)
Briary Primary School, Herne Bay

# Maradona's Best

**M** ummy, I love you.
**A** pples from the trees.
**R** ap me out!
**A** dog likes me.
**D** og is sniffing me.
**O** i, oi, oi, don't steal my money.
**N** ap, nap, nap, please.
**A** grown-up is playing football.

**B** each ball I can play.
**E** ach has counters.
**S** uspicious, *mmmm!*
**T** uck your seat belt, please.

## Archie Moulton (6)
Briary Primary School, Herne Bay

# Lemonade

**L** ove lemonade.
**E** at it with my fish and chips.
**M** y brother eats it every day.
**O** h, I don't drink it every day.
**N** o, I didn't say I do not like drinking it.
**A** t the hotel we get lemonade.
**D** urable for a big breakfast.
**E** veryone would like lemonade.

## Eli Offormezle (7)
Briary Primary School, Herne Bay

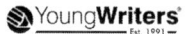

# Immanuel's Poem

I am very intelligent and clever.
M y toys are fun to play with.
M agnificent days at school.
A mazing days come to life.
N ice behaviour every day.
U nbelievably nice to my parents.
E ntering competitions is fun.
L ovely to my mum.

## Immanuel Osagie (7)
Briary Primary School, Herne Bay

# This Is Me

**T** his is my favourite teddy.
**H** appy reading a book.
**I** love my two brothers.
**S** pots are my favourite pattern.

**I** love my little baby cousin.
**S** wimming lessons on Thursdays.

**M** e in my bed.
**E** zme is my friend.

## Poppy Gaute (6)
Briary Primary School, Herne Bay

# Myself

T wo brothers.
H appy to have friends.
I love my mum and dad.
S ister is funny.

I like Mrs Huxley.
S pider-Man is good at climbing.

M y teachers make me happy and learn.
E le makes me happy and smiley.

## Tillie Griggs (6)
Briary Primary School, Herne Bay

# This Is Me

**T** wo older brothers.
**H** appy to have friends.
**I** love my guinea pigs.
**S** uperstar at reading.

**I** always love my family.
**S** paghetti is my favourite food.

**M** y family loves me.
**E** veryone is my favourite.

**Phoebe Goldstraw (7)**
Briary Primary School, Herne Bay

# This Is Me

T wo brothers.
H appy with Anya.
I love my dog.
S uuperstar at phonics.

I like Diya as a friend.
S paghetti is my favourite food.

M iss Akers is my best friend.
E verything is comfy.

## Amber Arnold (6)
Briary Primary School, Herne Bay

# Unicorn

**U** nicorns are the best.
**N** ice unicorns I love the best.
**I** think they're adorable and cute.
**C** orn is good for them.
**O** nce I saw them.
**R** ainbows are made from unicorns.
**N** ever ever see a unicorn!

**Minsa Reman (7)**
Briary Primary School, Herne Bay

# Happy

**L** ike friends.
**I** love my sisters.
**A** sister is chasing me.
**M** aths star.

**A** sister is hitting me.
**L** ove Dad.
**L** ove Mum.
**E** ggs are a good food.
**N** ice people.

## Liam Allen (6)
Briary Primary School, Herne Bay

# Volcanoes

**V** olcanoes explode.
**O** xygen goes out.
**L** ava flows out.
**C** louds of ash form.
**A** sh clouds.
**N** o one can survive
**O** n the volcano.
**E** xploding.
**S** ome rocks spill out.

**Theo Cooley (5)**
Briary Primary School, Herne Bay

# This Is Me

T eatime.
H ot chocolate.
I love my dad.
S helby is my sister.

I love my dad.
S isters are the best.

M y family love holidays.
E veryone loves me.

## MJ Wheeler (6)
Briary Primary School, Herne Bay

# Netball

**N** oisy cheering.
**E** veryone playing in the sun.
**T** hey need a ticket.
**B** ouncing balls up and down.
**A** winning team.
**L** ove playing.
**L** ove dribbling.

**Max Johnson (7)**
Briary Primary School, Herne Bay

# Beach

**B** irds splashing in the shallow water.
**E** veryone is swimming.
**A** seagull swoops on someone's chips.
**C** rabs scuttling sideways.
**H** appy day on the beach.

**Aubrey Hornsey (6)**
Briary Primary School, Herne Bay

# This Is Me

**T** oys.
**H** appy.
**I** love Mum.
**S** wimming.

**I** ce cream in the sun.
**S** weets.

**M** um.
**E** xcellent at handwriting.

## Max Hart (6)
Briary Primary School, Herne Bay

# Beach

**B** askets of picnic food.
**E** veryone is swimming in the sea.
**A** n umbrella blew away.
**C** louds were in the blue sky.
**H** appy because I make sandcastles.

## Jack Brookes (7)
Briary Primary School, Herne Bay

# Happy

**H** aving fun.
**A** lways smiling.
**P** laying with my brother.
**P** laying with my brother and sister.
**Y** es, doing things together.

**Taylor Clark-Jones (7)**
Briary Primary School, Herne Bay

# Me

**J** ust jogging.
**E** xciting.
**S** nake lover.
**S** pectacular.
**I** gloo lover.
**C** amel rider.
**A** mazing writer.

## Jessica Kelly (7)
Briary Primary School, Herne Bay

# Happy

**H** aving fun with my sister.
**A** lways kind to people.
**P** laying with my mum.
**P** laying in the park.
**Y** es, playing together.

**Lillie-Mae Guida (6)**
Briary Primary School, Herne Bay

# Happy

**H** aving fun with Harper.
**A** lways having fun.
**P** laying with my friends.
**P** layings games on my tablet.
**Y** es, this is me.

## Poppy Tambling (6)
Briary Primary School, Herne Bay

# Blaze

**B** laze is a boy.
**L** iverpool is the best.
**A** swimming boy.
**Z** igzags everywhere.
**E** ngland football supporter.

**Blaze Blackwood (6)**
Briary Primary School, Herne Bay

# Beach

**B** uckets and spades packed.
**E** veryone excited.
**A** rrived happily.
**C** rabs nipping.
**H** ot sun beaming down.

## Evie-Sue Weller (6)
Briary Primary School, Herne Bay

# Logan

**L** istening to Fortnite.
**O** range juice is my favourite.
**G** oing to football.
**A** lways playing.
**N** ever sad.

## Logan Bennett (7)
Briary Primary School, Herne Bay

# Happy

**H** aving fun.
**A** lways smiling.
**P** laying with friends.
**P** laying with our mum and dad.
**Y** es, this is me.

## Harper Robb (6)
Briary Primary School, Herne Bay

# Happy

**H** elpful.
**A** lways kind.
**P** laying with my brothers.
**P** laying with my toys.
**Y** es, this is me.

## Jaxon Wells
Briary Primary School, Herne Bay

# Happy

**H** elpful.
**A** lways smiling.
**P** laying with my sisters.
**P** lanning birthdays.
**Y** es, this is me.

## Elyshia Lee (7)
Briary Primary School, Herne Bay

# Happy

**H** elpful always.
**A** lways kind.
**P** laying with my sister.
**P** erfect smile.
**Y** es, this is me.

## Anuja Sawade (6)
Briary Primary School, Herne Bay

# Happy

**H** aving fun with my sister.
**A** mazing.
**P** laying with my toys.
**P** erfect.
**Y** es, this is me.

## Bella Guly (6)
Briary Primary School, Herne Bay

# Rabbit

**R** unner.
**A** pple eater.
**B** ubble blower.
**B** anana.
**I** ce cream eater.
**T** ickles.

## Jamsine Warren-Davies (7)
Briary Primary School, Herne Bay

# Happy

**H** aving fun.
**A** lways happy.
**P** laying with Anuja.
**P** layful.
**Y** ay, playing all the time.

## Chloe Osbourn (6)
Briary Primary School, Herne Bay

# Callum

**C** aterpillar.
**A** pple
**L** oki.
**L** ogan.
**U** mbrella
**M** y 7th birthday party.

## Callum O'Shea (6)
Briary Primary School, Herne Bay

# Happy

**H** elpful.
**A** lways happy.
**P** laying with everyone.
**P** erfect.
**Y** es, this is me.

## Maisie-Anne Arnold (7)
Briary Primary School, Herne Bay

# Loki

**L** ucky
**O** range is my favourite colour.
**K** ind and
**I** maginative.

## Loki Read (7)
Briary Primary School, Herne Bay

# Joey

**J** elly.
**O** range.
**E** lephant.
**Y** o-yo.

## Joey Dalten-Bower
Briary Primary School, Herne Bay

# Cat

**C** uddly cat.
**A** dorable cat.
**T** ap the cat.

## Elsie Gray (7)
Briary Primary School, Herne Bay

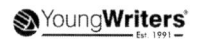

# Dog

**D** elightful.
**O** ne of a kind.
**G** race.

## Daisy Hillier (5)
Briary Primary School, Herne Bay

# My Rainbow

R eading loads of books is fun
A mazing at gymnastics
I love animals
N ice and loving
B ig heart
O ranges are my favourite fruit
W ow, these make me happy.

## Olive Eaves (7)
Chilham St Mary's CE Primary School, Chilham

# Dolly

**D** olly is so fluffy
**O** live is my friend
**L** .O.L.s are my favourite toys
**L** emons are disgusting
**Y** ummy bubblegum ice cream is my favourite.

## Eleana Barton Slade (7)
Chilham St Mary's CE Primary School, Chilham

# Teddy

**T** heme parks are fun
**E** njoy playing with my mum
**D** inky is my fluffy dog
**D** oing reading with Daddy
**Y** ummy spaghetti bolognese.

**Poppy Atkin (6)**
Chilham St Mary's CE Primary School, Chilham

# Happy

**H** igh up in the sky
**A** pples are my favourite thing to eat
**P** laying is my favourite
**P** aint with me
**Y** ellow sun makes me happy.

## Martha Wright (5)
Chilham St Mary's CE Primary School, Chilham

# Bella

**B** ella is cute
**E** rin is my sister
**L** .O.L.s are my favourite toy
**L** ollies are my fave
**A** sleepover with Holly and Eleana.

## Phoebe Shoults (7)
Chilham St Mary's CE Primary School, Chilham

# Autumn

**A** mazing colours
**U** nder the tree you will find conkers
**T** rees are losing their leaves
**U** nbelievable colours all around
**M** iles of crops
**N** ext is winter when we might get snow.

## Autumn Millard (6)
Emersons Green Primary School, Emersons Green

# Creative Archie

**A** good student
**R** unning club is his favourite club
**C** limbing is his favourite thing
**H** e likes 3D jigsaws
**I** like ice cream
**E** licie is my sister.

## Archie Savage (6)
Emersons Green Primary School, Emersons Green

# My Favourite Fairy

**F** airy is my favourite
**A** nd I love her so much
**I** n a round house she lives
**R** eally delicate wings
**Y** ou would love her too.

## Imani May Teddy (6)
Emersons Green Primary School, Emersons Green

# Star

**S** hine so bright
**T** winkle in the sky
**A** ll around the world
**R** ockets blast by.

## Sofia Beard (6)
Emersons Green Primary School, Emersons Green

# Alba

**A** lways happy
**L** ove unicorns
**B** est at climbing
**A** nd being a good friend.

## Aiba Davey (6)
Emersons Green Primary School, Emersons Green

# Holiday Vibes

H appy days
O n the beach
L ying down sunbathing
I ce cream with sprinkles
D iving into the sea
A mazing sunset
Y ellow sand

V ery hot day
I n a caravan
B usy donkey rides
E xciting trip
S wimming in the pool.

**Kelisia Mellis (7)**
Goodyers End Primary School, Bedworth

# Tamara

**T** rampoline is fun
**A** mazing to jump around
**M** any times in the air
**A** nd be happy at it
**R** ed Kangaroo Park is
**A** lways fun.

## Tamara Adeyemo (4)
Goodyers End Primary School, Bedworth

# Robyn

**R** eading is my skill
**O** n the swings is my happiness
**B** oats in the bath are funny
**Y** oghurt? Yes! Yummy
**N** ever. Enough. Stickers.

## Robyn Rule (5)
Goodyers End Primary School, Bedworth

# All About Me

R unning around in the town
I nsects chasing me all around
L ooking and laughing
E veryone smiling
Y um yum.

## Riley Barson (5)
Goodyers End Primary School, Bedworth

## Polar Express

**T** oy trains
**R** eal trains
**A** ll aboard
**I** love trains
**N** ow I hear a whistle
**S** lowly pulling away.

## Dylan Savage (6)
Goodyers End Primary School, Bedworth

# Honey

**H** ow I love ice cream
**O** range is my favourite
**N** o more cream
**E** at your food
**Y** ou must rest all the time.

## Ariel Nwagwu (7)
Goodyers End Primary School, Bedworth

# This Is Me, Thomas

**T** op of the class
**H** ard-working
**O** ne of a kind
**M** aths master
**A** lways helpful
**S** uper speller.

## Thomas Lewis (6)
Goodyers End Primary School, Bedworth

# This Is Me

**S** ummer days I love
**I** ce cream I like to lick
**Y** ellow is my favourite colour
**A** stronauts are cool.

## Siya Yadav (5)
Goodyers End Primary School, Bedworth

# Candy

**C** runchy and chewy
**A** wesome
**N** ice and sweet
**D** elightful and delicious
**Y** ummy treat.

**Ranjot Singh (7)**
Goodyers End Primary School, Bedworth

# Party

**P** ink presents
**A** big cake
**R** obot dance
**T** he party is amazing
**Y** ay, fun!

## Maisie Gleeson (4)
Goodyers End Primary School, Bedworth

## Zoo

**Z** ebras can run fast
**O** wls come out at night
**O** ur mum cooks good food.

## Alexis Nwagwu (7)
Goodyers End Primary School, Bedworth

# The Queen

**Q** ueen Elizabeth has a bubbly personality.
**U** nited Kingdom is the Queen's place.
**E** ach day Queen Elizabeth sits on her chair.
**E** njoy your planning.
**N** ervous Queen having her coronation.

**E** choes in the palace.
**L** arge room she sits on the throne.
**I** think she loves her palace.
**Z** igzag the palace goes.
**A** beautiful palace she has.
**B** osses the assistants to give her stuff.
**E** veryone wants to see the Queen.
**T** aking her corgis for a walk.
**H** er coronation was in 1952 in Westminster Abbey.

## Carlos Etayo Sanchez (5)
Holy Cross RC Primary School, Fulham

# The Queen

Q ueen Elizabeth is in love with corgis.
U pon the Queen's roof there are gold birds.
E lizabeth sat on Edward's chair.
E lizabeth enjoyed her coronation.
N early the Queen is ninety-six years old.

R ain drops on the Queen.
E lizabeth was married.
I went to the park.
G reat Queen.
N ice Queen.

**Hesham Dajani (6)**
Holy Cross RC Primary School, Fulham

# Jesus

**J** esus, we love you
**E** ven if you did die.
**S** acrificing yourself as a Messiah
**U** ntil you got sacrificed.
**S** acrificing is bad because everybody loves you.

**H** appy days because of you.
**A** day is beautiful because of you.
**P** raying for you is good.
**P** raising you is good.
**Y** ou are the life of God.

## Eden Assefa (6)
Holy Cross RC Primary School, Fulham

# The Best Teacher!

**B** arbados is the best country I've ever seen!
**O** n the plane, I watched some videos.
**G** o and do your work.
**A** lways bring your swimming kit.
**L** ook out for colours.
**S** tay together.
**K** now what to do.
**I** know that you always have to listen to the teachers.

## Hannah Macias (6)
Holy Cross RC Primary School, Fulham

# My Teacher Is Smart!

**M** y favourite teacher ever!
**I** ngenious.
**S** he smells very nice!
**S** he is skilled.

**B** est teacher ever!
**O** n time every day!
**G** reat at teaching!
**A** mazing at helping us.
**L** ovely.
**S** mart.
**K** ind.
**I** love you!

## Claudia Nortes (7)
Holy Cross RC Primary School, Fulham

# Best Ms Bogalski

**M** ost beautiful.
**S** he shines very brightly.

**B** est at baking.
**O** n time every time.
**G** reatest teacher of all time.
**A** lways amazing.
**L** oving person.
**S** eriously so cool.
**K** ind to all who encounter her.
**I** love you!

## Isabella Newell (7)
Holy Cross RC Primary School, Fulham

## My Lovely Teacher

**B** est teacher in the world.
**O** MG, she is such a lovely teacher.
**G** reat teacher I know.
**A** mazing teacher.
**L** oving girl or teacher.
**S** ometimes she's silly or funny.
**K** ind, honest, caring girl or teacher.
**I** ntelligent and nice girl.

### Jessica Osorio Tavares (7)
Holy Cross RC Primary School, Fulham

# The Queen

**Q** ueen Elizabeth loves corgis, she has corgis at her home.
**U** pon Queen Elizabeth's rooftop, there are golden chickens.
**E** lizabeth got married to Prince Philip.
**E** dward is so angry every Monday.
k **N** ights are in the castle because they protect the palace.

**Amelia Lovett (5)**
Holy Cross RC Primary School, Fulham

# Basketball

**B** all.
**A** ll the people having fun.
**S** o many goals.
**K** eeps going on.
**E** veryone excited.
**T** ossing the ball towards the hoop.
**B** all in the net.
**A** ll people scoring.
**L** oud noises.
**L** aughing and cheering.

## Benjamin Smith (7)
Holy Cross RC Primary School, Fulham

## Masters Of Colour

**R** ain comes from clouds sky.
**A** lways goes to the ground without stopping
**I** t can even fall on the roof.
**N** ever unhappy. No, no!
**B** eautiful colours and weather.
**O** n a day sometimes it rains.
**W** orking beautifully to stand out!

## Adewunmi (7)
Holy Cross RC Primary School, Fulham

# The Queen

**Q** ueen Elizabeth loves corgis.
**U** pon Queen Elizabeth's head is a crown.
**E** dward's brothers call Queen Elizabeth Mommy.
**E** dward's chair is what Queen Elizabeth loves.
**N** ervous Queen Elizabeth at her coronation.

## Hallie Morgan (5)
Holy Cross RC Primary School, Fulham

# Queen Elizabeth

**Q** ueen Elizabeth is happy when she sees a dog and her favourite is a corgi.
**U** nited Kingdom is what the Queen rules.
**E** ach queen wears a crown.
**E** lizabeth is the Queen's real name.
**N** ever shout at the Queen.

## Leila Nuqui (6)
Holy Cross RC Primary School, Fulham

# The Queen

**Q** ueen Elizabeth loves corgis so much.
**U** nited Kingdom is Queen Elizabeth's home where she lives.
**E** dward holds Queen
**E** lizabeth's cape when she was getting married.
**N** othing will hurt the amazing Queen.

## Viktoria Hoxha (6)
Holy Cross RC Primary School, Fulham

# The Queen

**Q** ueen Elizabeth is coming to the
**U** nited Kingdom. She was born in 1926, her name
**E** lizabeth the Second.
**E** verybody was waiting for her to be crowned at Westminster Abbey.
**N** othing to worry about, you are safe.

**Valery Astaiza (6)**
Holy Cross RC Primary School, Fulham

# Science Is Very Good

**S** mart.
**C** urious.
**I** ntelligent.
**E** xperiments are very fun.
**N** ever get questions wrong.
**T** alk a lot.
**I** ntelligent at maths and science.
**S** cience master.
**T** alkative.

## Amen Benyam (7)
Holy Cross RC Primary School, Fulham

# Going To The Beach

**B** ogalski and Miss Newbury at the beach.
**E** xcellent at making sandcastles.
**A** mazing at looking for good seashells.
**C** hocolate is the second-best ice cream on the beach.
**H** undreds of stones at the beach.

## Jacob Duffield (7)
Holy Cross RC Primary School, Fulham

# The Queen

**Q** ueen Elizabeth loves corgis.
**U** pon Elizabeth's head sits a crown.
**E** dward's chair is sat on by the Queen.
**E** njoy your Platinum Jubilee.
**N** ervously she enters Westminster Abbey for her crown.

## Zach Wyatt (6)
Holy Cross RC Primary School, Fulham

## Jesus

**J** esus, God sent you from heaven.
**E** veryone has been waiting for you.
**S** acrificing yourself, as the Messiah.
**U** ntil you rise again, you will be in heaven with your father.
**S** ee you someday Jesus!

**Oliver Dobbs (6) & Teresa**
Holy Cross RC Primary School, Fulham

## The Queen

**Q** ueen Elizabeth everyone is waiting for you!
**U** nited Kingdom is even here!
**E** veryone is looking for you now.
**E** veryone loves you because you are the Queen.
**N** othing will harm you I promise!

### Nina Ribeiro Hill (6)
Holy Cross RC Primary School, Fulham

# The Queen

**Q** ueen Elizabeth the 2nd is protected by soldiers.
**U** pon her rooftop is a flag.
**E** verybody wants to see the Queen.
**E** lizabeth has four children.
**N** early seventy years she has ruled over us.

**Mason Kirby-Taylor (5)**
Holy Cross RC Primary School, Fulham

# The Queen

**Q** ueen Elizabeth is the boss of my kingdom.
**U** pon her roof a flag flies.
**E** verybody wants to see the Queen.
**E** ngland is where she lives.
**N** early seventy years she has ruled over us.

## Blanca Solans (6)
Holy Cross RC Primary School, Fulham

# Champions Of Europe

**C** lever at scoring goals.
**H** elpful team.
**E** mpathy when they win.
**L** eague champions.
**S** o supportive.
**E** xtraordinarily good at tackling.
**A** lways on schedule.

## Alexander Bracke (6)
Holy Cross RC Primary School, Fulham

# The Queen

**Q** ueen Elizabeth loves perfume.
**U** pon the castle there are gems.
**E** very day Queen Elizabeth sees corgis.
**E** ach day the Queen watches TV.
**N** ervous Queen is fifty-nine years old.

## Elnathan Elias (6)
Holy Cross RC Primary School, Fulham

# Champions Of Europe

  **C** helsea is the best.
c **H** ampions of Europe.
  **E** xtremely good team.
  **L** eague champions.
  **S** o good.
  **E** xtremely good at scoring.
  **A** mazing Mason Mount.

**Arthur Charles Farrell Dewfall (6)**
Holy Cross RC Primary School, Fulham

# The Queen

**Q** uick, Queen Elizabeth, the
**U** nited Kingdom is waiting for you to
**E** nter Westminster Abbey,
**E** verybody will come to see your coronation.
**N** othing will scare you!

## Evelina Juncu (6) & Sara (6)
Holy Cross RC Primary School, Fulham

## Jesus

**J** esus save the Queen.
**E** verybody in the UK is waiting to fight.
**"S** top!" said Jesus
**U** ntil the fighting was over.
**S** o Jesus saved the world.

### Romano Mason (6)
Holy Cross RC Primary School, Fulham

# All About Stars In The Sky

**S** mell like flowers.
**T** winkle like a moon in the sky.
**A** mazing at being bright.
**R** eally like the kind, loving Queen.
**S** mart at maths and teaching it.

## Kitty Hughes (6)
Holy Cross RC Primary School, Fulham

# The Queen

**Q** ueen Elizabeth can I see you?
**U** se the door lock.
**E** veryone is waiting for you.
**E** verybody is looking for you.
**N** othing will harm your children.

**Marcela Marcatto de Abreu (6)**
Holy Cross RC Primary School, Fulham

# The Queen

**Q** ueen Elizabeth is a good queen.
**U** nder us, the Queen lies.
**E** lizabeth is her name.
**E** very day she has a Red Box.
**N** early her 100th birthday.

## Paul Patrick Lloyd (6)
Holy Cross RC Primary School, Fulham

# The Queen

**Q** ueen Elizabeth was born in the UK in 1926.
**U** nder all the sky.
**E** veryone will love you.
**E** veryone will celebrate.
**N** othing will scare you.

**Luna Petrillo (6)**
Holy Cross RC Primary School, Fulham

# The World

**W** hat is this world?
**O** ur time to pray to God.
**R** ejoice in our happiness and love.
**L** ike what we do.
**D** on't throw rubbish on the floor.

**Harrison Mbilika-Edafioka (6)**
Holy Cross RC Primary School, Fulham

# World

W hat will the world do?
O ur world is a planet that is made for
R ejoicing and happiness.
L ike the world and remember
D o keep it safe!

## Sebastian (6)
Holy Cross RC Primary School, Fulham

# The Queen

**Q** ueen, they need you in the
**U** nited Kingdom.
**E** ver so pretty when you
**E** nter Westminster Abbey.
**N** ever be alone because you are safe.

## Constance (6)
Holy Cross RC Primary School, Fulham

# The Amazing Maria

**M** y sister is the best.
**A** mazing at school.
**R** elies on me.
**I** t is amazing to have her as my sister.
**A** mazingly good at comforting me.

**Isabel Fontes Cardoso (6)**
Holy Cross RC Primary School, Fulham

# The World

**W** hat is the world?
**O** ur world has wild animals.
**R** un and look at the grassland of the world.
**L** ove the world,
**D** on't litter.

## Conor Byrne (6)
Holy Cross RC Primary School, Fulham

# My Favourite Brother

**E** xcited, very excited
**T** hat he loves football.
**H** ates vegetables
**A** nd loves to play with our cat.
**N** ever gives up on football.

**Alex Frain (7)**
Holy Cross RC Primary School, Fulham

# The World

**W** hat is the world we live on?
**O** ur place to pray to God.
**R** ejoice in our happiness.
**L** ike what we do.
**D** on't throw litter.

## Leandro Pyaralli Salvador (6)
Holy Cross RC Primary School, Fulham

# Skiing

**S** o cold.
**K** ite flying after skiing.
**I** nside it's so warm.
**I** love it!
**N** ever gets old.
**G** ets better every day.

**Joseph Jackson (7)**
Holy Cross RC Primary School, Fulham

# The World

**W** hy do we need the world?
**O** ur world is nice.
**R** ejoice in our world.
**L** oving our world is important.
**D** on't dig it up.

## Noah McGuirk (6)
Holy Cross RC Primary School, Fulham

# The World

**W** hat is the world?
**O** ur planet to live on.
**R** ejoice, our happiness is here.
**L** ike the world,
**D** on't dig it up!

## Afonso (5)
Holy Cross RC Primary School, Fulham

# The World

**W** hat is the world?
**O** ur planet to live on.
**R** ejoice in our happiness.
**L** ike what we do.
**D** on't dig it up!

## Felix Ihlenfeld (6)
Holy Cross RC Primary School, Fulham

# Amazing Molly Is The Best Girl!

**M** ost amazing sibling.
**O** lly went to her house.
**L** ollipop girl.
**L** olly is amazing.
**Y** ou are amazing.

**Maisy Power (6)**
Holy Cross RC Primary School, Fulham

# Best

**B** ad at handwriting.
**E** xcellent at basketball.
**S** uper at football.
**T** ennis is one of my favourite sports.

## Foucauld Gaudy (6)
Holy Cross RC Primary School, Fulham

# I Love To Learn

I love to ride my bike.

L iteracy is very fun!
O ceans are a good thing to learn about in geography.
V iolins and pianos - I love music!
E very day at school I learn something new.

T eachers help students learn.
O f all the things in the world, I love learning about nature.

L earning is great to do.
E very night I read fantastic books.
A dding or subtracting, maths is brilliant.
R E is where we learn about religions.
N othing can stop us when we learn loads!

**Jenny O'Brien (5)**
Marlcliffe Community Primary School, Sheffield

# My Favourites

**M** aking things with Lego.
**Y** ellow.

**F** unfairs and freak out rides.
**A** bigail, Edie and Jesse.
**V** isiting Nanny and Grandad at the seaside.
**O** utside fun and games.
**U** nder my bed den.
**R** iding my bike.
**I** love eating jellies.
**T** V watching.
**E** ating pasta and pizza.
**S** pace, especially Neptune.

## Dexter Bott (7)
Marlcliffe Community Primary School, Sheffield

# Gymnastics

**G** oing on beam having fun.
**Y** ou can see me swing on the bar.
**M** any things to do.
**N** ew things to learn and do.
**A** lways try your best and believe in yourself.
**S** plits we practise every lesson.
**T** uck jumps are really hard.
**I** n warm-up we do a bridge.
**C** an you do a handstand too?
**S** o come and have fun with me!

**Poppy Sweeney (7)**
Marlcliffe Community Primary School, Sheffield

# Creative Me

**C** ats, unicorns and rainbows are some of my favourite things.
**R** eally love to read and write.
**E** very day I like to draw.
**A** rt and crafts are my favourite things to do!
**T** ie-dyeing T-shirts is really fun!
**I** want to be a teacher when I grow up.
**V** ery good dancer.
**E** verything about me is creative and kind.

## Zoe Nall (6)
Marlcliffe Community Primary School, Sheffield

# Bring On The Brownies

**B** rownies is my favourite club.
**R** emember to always keep the Brownie Guide Law.
**O** ur group is welcome to everybody.
**W** e wear our badges with pride.
**N** othing is never not fun.
**I** promise I will do my best.
**E** very week we do something different.
**S** erve the Queen and my community!

## Georgia Neasmith (7)
Marlcliffe Community Primary School, Sheffield

# House

**H** ome is the best place and a safe place.
**O** n a rainy day, it doesn't spoil the fun.
**U** nder the shelter, it is not fun.
**S** ome houses are different and I do not care.
**E** mpty dishes or clean and our house is a lovely place. I want to live around my family forever. I am happy. I want to stay.

## Harriet Grayson (6)
Marlcliffe Community Primary School, Sheffield

# Me And Diabetes

**D** iabetes, Type 1 since I was three.
**I** eat lots of fruit and vegetables.
**A** tummy without a real pancreas.
**B** lood tests every day.
**E** very day I am very good.
**T** oo many sweets make me poorly.
**E** ach day I go to school.
**S** uperstar is one of the best words to me.

## Alice Hague (6)
Marlcliffe Community Primary School, Sheffield

# Rockstar

**R** ocking out on stage.
**O** n my stadium tour.
**C** rowds cheering and having fun.
**K** icking my guitar because I'm crazy.
**S** inging into my microphone.
**T** en amazing tracks on my album.
**A** wesome instruments in my band.
**R** eal-life pop star. It's my destiny!

## Theo Brown (7)
Marlcliffe Community Primary School, Sheffield

# Jubilee

**J** oin the fun with the Queen.
**U** nbelievable things the Queen does.
**B** ig parties are planned.
**I** s known as the Platinum Jubilee.
**L** et's celebrate the Queen's 70th anniversary
**E** lizabeth II is our Queen.
**E** verybody clap your hands.

## Darcie Thompson (7)
Marlcliffe Community Primary School, Sheffield

# Friends

**F** riends are loving and sweet.
**R** eady for you to come
**I** nside and ready for your surprise party.
**E** xactly as I said it, friends are helpful.
**N** ever late for you.
**D** efinitely, you love your friends.
**S** ee things in you.

## Matilda Stone (7)
Marlcliffe Community Primary School, Sheffield

# Happy

**H** ooray, hooray, it's our holiday!
**A** hh I see a jellyfish, quick, run away.
**P** retty pink pigs on a farm, so cute!
**P** ond water splashing on me, I dry quickly in the sun.
**Y** ay, I'm going home to see my friends!

**Jesse Akers (7)**
Marlcliffe Community Primary School, Sheffield

# Baking Is Fun

**B** aking delicious foods
**A** nd having lots of fun.
**K** eeping it for your party.
**I** nviting all your friends.
**N** eeding all your happiness never ever ends.
**G** rateful for the company and all the tasty treats.

## Amelie Callaghan (7)
Marlcliffe Community Primary School, Sheffield

# Joyful

**J** oy is all the colours!
**O** h how would we live without joy?
**Y** ou gain loads of energy!
**F** aster and faster, your heart gets faster
**U** ntil it's pure happiness
**L** ike the smell of candy canes!

## River Savage (6)
Marlcliffe Community Primary School, Sheffield

# My Mummy

**M** any DVDs I stay up to watch together.
**U** p in the trees out of the house, walks on the common.
**M** any toys my mummy buys for me.
**M** ummy is the best.
**Y** ummy food I make with my mummy.

**Ava Bothamley (7)**
Marlcliffe Community Primary School, Sheffield

# My Home

M y chimney is tall.
Y ou are welcome.

H appy memories passing by.
O nly friendly people around.
M y family is great.
E veryone passing by.

## Dominic Hague (7)
Marlcliffe Community Primary School, Sheffield

# My Cat

**M** eowing loudly at me.
**Y** oung kittens to old cats.

**C** urled up in a ball
**A** s a cat would do, licking its paws.
**T** urning on its belly to back.

## Anna Brownley (6)
Marlcliffe Community Primary School, Sheffield

# Made In Sheffield

**S** omeone is polishing steel.
**T** he steel is silver.
**E** very item is shiny.
**E** very item takes a long time to make.
**L** ots of things are made of steel.

## Emmiie Perry (7)
Marlcliffe Community Primary School, Sheffield

# Train

**T** hey pull passenger coaches.
**R** un on tracks.
**A** lways arrive on time.
**I** n and out of tunnels.
**N** ever derails.

## Lenny Anglesea-French (6)
Marlcliffe Community Primary School, Sheffield

# Godzilla

**G** etting ready to get food.
**O** h, how small his space is!
**D** oing things he needs.
**Z** *zzz, shhhh!! He's asleep.*
**I** love him, he's very important.
**L** ittle feet stepping on sand.
**L** ittle cage for him.
**A** little rankin named Godzilla.

**Jacob Leither (6)**
Purbrook Infant School, Purbrook

# Hungry

**H** am is a nice thing to eat.
**U** ncover a bowl of pasta so I can eat it.
**N** uts because at Christmas time you crack them.
**G** ravy on my roast dinner so they taste good.
**R** avenous I am for apples.
**Y** ellow potatoes with my roast dinners because they taste marvellous.

## Lilly-Anne Fry (7)
Purbrook Infant School, Purbrook

# Darcie E

**D** aring, I am very brave.
**A** spirational, I am wildly creative.
**R** ocking, I'm cool.
**C** aring, I like to help people.
**I** ntelligent, I like maths and English.
**E** nergetic, I am very sporty.

**E** nthusiastic, I love learning.

## Darcie Ellcome (7)
Purbrook Infant School, Purbrook

# Gymnast

**G** ym leads to strength.
**Y** ou means love.
**M** y mum loves flowers.
**N** ow I can do a fantastic bridge.
**A** t gymnastics, I'm getting better.
**S** carlett loves to stretch.
**T** he last time I went to gymnastics I had a good time.

## Scarlett Wright (7)
Purbrook Infant School, Purbrook

# Football

**F** eeling jealous because my brother stole my tablet.
**O** n my tablet I play games.
**O** n my birthday I like curry.
**T** elling a story is fun.
**B** usy as a bee.
**A** gentle boy.
**L** ovely but crazy.
**L** oved by my mum.

**Cusin Aji Joseph (7)**
Purbrook Infant School, Purbrook

# Travelling

**T** aming animals.
**R** owing in boats.
**A** rriving.
**V** ans.
**E** very morning sunshine.
**L** earning survival skills.
**L** eaping frogs.
**I** sla is my name.
**N** ice knitted jumper.
**G** oing home.

## Isla Dalgleish (6)
Purbrook Infant School, Purbrook

# Hayden

**H** ome is my safe place.
**A** ctivities are fun and I like to do archery.
**Y** ear's seasons are fun.
**D** raughts I love to play on a board.
**E** xplore, find out a lot of new things.
**N** athan my brother is ten and I love him.

**Hayden Jackson (7)**
Purbrook Infant School, Purbrook

# Charlie

**C** harlie is a small, kind boy.
**H** ilarious is Charlie's ability.
**A** dventurous is what I like.
**R** ight every day.
**L** ives for family.
**I** ntelligent, I know everything.
**E** legant, I'm just like a teacher.

## Charlie Shepherd (7)
Purbrook Infant School, Purbrook

# Sienna G

**S** ensible, I like to help my teacher.
**I** ntelligent, I know everything.
**E** legant, I'm just like a princess.
**N** ever afraid.
**N** ever naughty.
**A** lways kind.

**G** reat at being a friend.

## Sienna Gosden (7)
Purbrook Infant School, Purbrook

# Angel

**A** lways kind and thoughtful in school.
**N** ice, I care about people and my friends.
**G** reat at English and book talk.
**E** xciting about nearly everything.
**L** ove my teacher and my family.

## Angel Bailey (7)
Purbrook Infant School, Purbrook

# Friend

**F** lowers and weddings are the best.
**R** ide my bike.
**I** am Sophia.
**E** njoy playing.
**N** anny is lovely.
**D** addy is kind and I love him.

## Sophia Cork (7)
Purbrook Infant School, Purbrook

# Mason

**M** ason is really kind and happy.
**A** lways helpful and exciting.
**S** weet, sensible at listening.
**O** liver is my friend.
**N** ever gives up.

## Mason Saunders (7)
Purbrook Infant School, Purbrook

# My Cat Sooty

S ooty is very playful.
O range is not for Sooty.
O range is a fruit.
T ea is for Sooty.
Y our love and care, Sooty likes.

**Logan Martin (7)**
Purbrook Infant School, Purbrook

# Oscar

**O** ff is to on.
**S** ad is to happy.
**C** razy is to calm.
**A** nnoying is to brothers.
**R** ight is to left.

## Holly Ziya (7)
Purbrook Infant School, Purbrook

# Football

**F** oot hitting the ball.
**O** ops, they lost to nil.
**O** wn goal.
**T** ake the ball.
**B** rahim Diaz, footballer.
**A** rsenal's team is the best.
**L** eon Ronaldo play with Manchester.
**L** arge stadium.

**Rayan Bouje Llaba (7)**
St Mary's Catholic Primary School, London

# Maria

**M** y mum called me Maria and I like it.
**A** ctive forest girl, running and jumping and looking for sticks.
**R** eading My Naughty Little Sister book makes me laugh.
**I** love myself and I know how to love others.
**A** mazing me!

## Maria Pinnock (7)
St Mary's Catholic Primary School, London

# Soraiya

**S** uper fun I am.
**O** utdoors I love to play.
**R** unning around all day.
**A** lways exciting.
**I** love to look for creatures.
**"Y** ay," I say when I find them crawling
**A** round on the ground.

## Soraiya Borelly (6)
St Mary's Catholic Primary School, London

# Easter

**E** aster is here.
**A** hh, exciting day.
**S** how time to hide the eggs.
**T** ing, go to church on Sundays.
**E** ek, time to find the Easter eggs.
**R** abbit? Easter rabbit!

## Nayomi Solomon (7)
St Mary's Catholic Primary School, London

# Kamber

**K** ind and brave.
**A** brilliant mate.
**M** akes lots of friends.
**B** eing always great.
**E** nergetic and funny
**R** unning around.

## Kamber Tanai (7)
St Mary's Catholic Primary School, London

# Livia's Love

**L** ove in the world.
**I** love purple, people and playing.
**V** ery important news!
**I** love gymnastics
**A** nd my family too!

## Livia Moscatelli-Darroux (6)
St Mary's Catholic Primary School, London

# Love

**L** ollipops.
**O** range.
**V** ery nice people.
**E** veryone is loved.

## Jeremiah Komeh (6)
St Mary's Catholic Primary School, London

# Sraiyah

**S** cared of spiders.
**R** estaurants are my favourite.
**A** lovely friend.
**I** love school.
**Y** ellow is my favourite colour.
**A** lways working.
**H** ave a baby sister.

## Sraiyah Holmes (6)
St Michael's CE (Aided) Primary School, Tettenhall

# Gureet

**G** reat at dancing.
**U** nder the blanket is my favourite spot.
**R** unning is my favourite sport.
**E** ggs are my favourite food.
**E** xcellent at maths.
**T** he best at singing.

## Gureet Tutt (6)
St Michael's CE (Aided) Primary School, Tettenhall

# Oliver

**O** range is my favourite food.
**L** ove my mom and dad.
**I** t is my favourite season.
**V** ultures are my favourite bird.
**E** nergetic.
**R** ed is my favourite colour.

## Oliver Clarkson (6)
St Michael's CE (Aided) Primary School, Tettenhall

# Nathan

**N** ice to my sister.
**A** loving boy.
**T** he best at football.
**H** appy at my friends.
**A** good person.
**N** ice to my sister.

## Nathan Nurse (6)
St Michael's CE (Aided) Primary School, Tettenhall

# Etta

**E** nglish is my favourite.
**T** ulip and Clementine are my twin baby sisters.
**T** he best thing I'm good at is art.
**A** lovely friend.

## Etta Tillett (5)
St Michael's CE (Aided) Primary School, Tettenhall

# Hirah

**H** ate buttercups.
**I** love butterflies.
**R** uns fast all the time.
**A** lovely friend.
**H** ate sweets but not lollipops.

## Hirah Saeed (5)
St Michael's CE (Aided) Primary School, Tettenhall

# Rowan

**R** ed is my favourite colour.
**O** ften go to church.
**W** ill always work hard.
**A** lways at school.
**N** ever stop working.

## Rowan Douglas (6)
St Michael's CE (Aided) Primary School, Tettenhall

# Shahin

**S** port player.
**H** appy.
**A** lways caring.
**H** elps people.
**I** like red.
**N** ever touches spiders.

## Shahin Khaja (6)
St Michael's CE (Aided) Primary School, Tettenhall

# Carter

**C** hatty.
**A** kind child.
**R** unner.
**T** urning around is fun.
**E** nergetic.
**R** acing with my dad.

## Carter Bailey (5)
St Michael's CE (Aided) Primary School, Tettenhall

# Lucas

**L** ove my dad.
**U** nited is my favourite team.
**C** an run fast.
**A** good singer.
**S** o good at football.

## Lucas Bromley (5)
St Michael's CE (Aided) Primary School, Tettenhall

# Jaxon

**J** oyful.
**A** loving friend.
**X** ylophones are fun.
**O** ranges are my favourite fruit.
**N** ever scared.

## Jaxon Durnall (5)
St Michael's CE (Aided) Primary School, Tettenhall

# Mary

**M** y sister is Phoebe.
**A** lovely friend.
**R** aspberries are my favourite.
**Y** ellow is my favourite colour.

## Mary Evans (6)
St Michael's CE (Aided) Primary School, Tettenhall

# Lexi

**L** ove spiders.
**E** xcited to go to the water park.
**X** -ray when I swallowed a 2p coin.
**I** love running.

## Lexi Bowen (5)
St Michael's CE (Aided) Primary School, Tettenhall

# Pearl

**P** retty.
**E** nergetic.
**A** lovely friend.
**R** aspberries, my favourite fruit.
**L** ively.

## Pearl Brown (6)
St Michael's CE (Aided) Primary School, Tettenhall

# Noah

**N** ice.
**O** range is my favourite fruit.
**A** lways kind.
**H** appy when I go to castles.

## Noah Jimenez-Kaul (6)
St Michael's CE (Aided) Primary School, Tettenhall

# Avni

**A** lovely friend.
**V** ery good at swimming.
**N** ice friend.
**I** hate spiders.

## Avni Puri (6)
St Michael's CE (Aided) Primary School, Tettenhall

# Aila

**A** lovely friend.
**I** love dogs.
**L** ove my parents.
**A** superstar.

## Aila Brown (6)
St Michael's CE (Aided) Primary School, Tettenhall

# Jap

**J** oyful.
**A** boxer.
**P** izza is my favourite food.

## Jap Sidhu (6)
St Michael's CE (Aided) Primary School, Tettenhall

# Young Writers Information

We hope you have enjoyed reading this book – and that you will continue to in the coming years.

If you're the parent or family member of an enthusiastic poet or story writer, do visit **www.youngwriters.co.uk/subscribe** and sign up to receive news, competitions, writing challenges and tips, activities and much, much more! There's lots to keep budding writers motivated!

If you would like to order further copies of this book, or any of our other titles, then please give us a call or order via your online account.

Young Writers
Remus House
Coltsfoot Drive
Peterborough
PE2 9BF
(01733) 890066
info@youngwriters.co.uk

Join in the conversation!
Tips, news, giveaways and much more!

YoungWritersUK   YoungWritersCW   youngwriterscw